MR. GARNER OF TEXAS

JOHN NANCE GARNER

MR. GARNER OF TEXAS

by Marquis James

THE BOBBS-MERRILL COMPANY
PUBLISHERS

INDIANAPOLIS   **NEW YORK**

CONTENTS

ILLUSTRATIONS

I

A BOY ON BLOSSOM PRAIRIE

I

A Boy on Blossom Prairie

G. T. T., meaning Gone to Texas, had a questionable ring in the Eighteen-Forties: too many people went to Texas a jump ahead of the sheriff. Old Texas lawyers still tell the story of the newcomer who sought out an attorney in their grandfather's day. It seems

11

that the immigrant's past had found him out and he was greatly, if needlessly, disturbed. The attorney thought he would have some fun.

"My friend," said he. "This is serious. My advice is to leave here before sundown."

"Leave," cried the astonished man. "Where'll I go? Ain't I in Texas now?"

Most of the settlers who headed for Sam Houston's republic in the early Forties without saying much about it were guilty of no more serious offense than to be caught on the short end of the financial collapse that had stunned the United States in 1837, closing an era of speculation in which too many persons had expected to get rich without working. In the spring of 1842 road-worn wagons made a line at the little Red River ferry at Fulton, Arkansas, gateway to the Promised Land. There were wagons of all sorts and travellers of all sorts, with a variety of stories to tell or not to tell.

In this motley caravan was a wagon driven by a woman. Six children, the youngest a baby, were with her. The story of Rebecca Walpole Garner, widow of John Nance Garner, was that

she sought a land of more spacious opportunity
for her three sons and three daughters. She had
come from Rutherford County, in Middle Tennessee, six hundred miles by the worst roads in
the Union that could be called roads at all. And
to Blossom Prairie would be a hundred miles
more.

Blossom Prairie, the widow's goal, was a bil-
lowing, fertile, natural "opening" in the jack oaks
of Red River County, miles across and ideal for
settlement. A family of her Walpole kinfolk—
descended from connections of the great English
prime minister—was already there. The Wal-
poles and their neighbors saw the widow and her
brood settled on a Blossom Prairie homestead; a
cabin raised, a crop put in, a new pioneering
enterprise begun. Rebecca Garner knew how to
manage. Her farm prospered, frontier fashion;
her boys and girls grew up, began to marry and
start homes of their own. Sam Houston saw his
republic come into the Union, and, his heart
heavy, he saw it go out with the Confederacy.
The youngest Garner boy, John Nance, junior,
named for the father who lay in a Tennessee

13

graveyard, became a cavalryman under Joe Wheeler.

In 1865 he rode back to Blossom Prairie, more fortunate than many southern fighting men in that he had a roof over his head. He married Sarah Guest, a daughter of a family of Blossom Prairie pioneers who formed a considerable clan thereabouts. Guests were the holders of local offices and titles and later they started a bank in the hamlet of Detroit. The ex-cavalryman and Sarah began married life in a squared-log cabin of their own where, on November 22, 1869, a son was born. They named him John Nance Garner, for his father and his grandfather.

John grew up in that log house, one of six brothers and sisters. He walked three miles to a country school which seldom kept open more than four months a year because the poverty of Reconstruction times was on the South. But John's real interest in the pursuit of learning was stimulated by an aunt, Kitty Garner, the only one of Rebecca's children who had not married. Aunt Kitty's love was a shelf of books, mostly histories. She got John interested and

Photograph by William Langley, Dallas, Texas

BIRTHPLACE OF JOHN N. GARNER, BLOSSOM PRAIRIE, RED RIVER COUNTY, TEXAS,
AS IT APPEARS TODAY

he went through the lot. What he read fired his mind to get out and see something of the world beyond the jack-bordered boundaries of Blossom Prairie, which was still pretty close to the jumping-off place. Ten miles north of the Garner farm the Red River, which except during the spring rise was more river bed than river, formed the boundary between Texas and the Choctaw Indian Nation, now southeastern Oklahoma.

Still, there was enough to do on Blossom Prairie to keep a boy out of mischief—something of an undertaking in the case of young John Garner, an undersized, blue-eyed, sandy-haired young one, active as a cat and full of the devil.

John Garner, the elder, made a good plain living off his farm. He kept two hired hands, one of whom, Francis Parker, slept with young John. They were great friends. On young John's eighth birthday Parker wanted to make the boy a present and at the same time to lighten a little his own work in the cotton field. He promised John five dollars if he would pick a hundred pounds of cotton before sundown. John was up picking cotton before the dew was off the bolls.

He weighed it in as he picked, before the bolls dried out. The result was a hundred and eight pounds. With the five dollars John bought a motherless mule colt which he raised and eventually sold for a hundred and fifty dollars. The stroke gratified John's father who banked the money, saying John should have it when old enough to strike out for himself in the world as he was always saying he was going to do.

John played shortstop on the Possum Trot baseball nine. Possum Trot was the name of a crossroads store in the Garner quarter of Blossom Prairie. The Possum Trot nine has passed into the domain of saga. Surviving players, John Garner among them, cannot recall that it ever lost a game. A counter-legend explains this by saying that when the score went against the Possum Trotters they would drop their gloves and resolve the fray in their favor with their fists.

At nineteen John made his first journey beyond the confines of the Red River Valley. He also took his first ride on a railroad train, and it was a long ride. John retraced the route by which his grandmother had come to Texas and at Nashville, Tennessee, he enrolled as a law student in Vanderbilt University. There it was that he found out how standards of scholarship vary. On Blossom Prairie he could exhibit definite academic attainments. No sum in arithmetic stumped him; he knew about everything that was in Aunt Kitty's history books; at Possum Trot's spelling bees and "literary" Friday evenings he was a master performer. But these accomplishments did not suffice a beginner in Vanderbilt's law course. Hopelessly unprepared for university work, John remained only a week.

Forty years later an archivist at Vanderbilt discovered John Garner's faint connection with that institution. Mr. Garner was offered an honorary degree of Doctor of Laws. In a grateful letter he declined saying that to accept would be unjust to those who had earned their diplomas in the regular way.

Despite the setback at Nashville John was not through trying to be a lawyer. He drew his hundred and fifty dollars and went to Clarksville, the county seat of Red River, and started to read law in the office of Captain M. L. Sims, an ex-

Confederate officer. He boarded for twelve dollars a month at the residence of Dr. Lane, late surgeon, C.S.A., thus eating up the proceeds of the sale of the motherless mule. When the money was gone John passed his examination for admission to the bar, the court waiving the fact that he was under twenty-one.

Settling down to practice the new attorney equipped his office with an iron safe which had been offered at a bargain. The only trouble was that Lawyer Garner seldom got hold of anything worth locking up. He ran for city attorney, but the other candidate nosed him out. After two years in Clarksville a doctor thumped John's chest and told him he had better try a dry climate.

On a dark night in December, 1892, John Garner stepped from a Galveston, Houston & San Antonio day coach at Uvalde, about fifty miles from the Rio Grande. In his pocket was $151.25—and it is like John to remember the twenty-five cents. A little horsehide-covered trunk contained the rest of the attorney's posses-

18

sions, including his law library. All but a few of Uvalde's sixteen hundred people were asleep. Gazing at the five or six lights which marked the town John Garner had a feeling that he would rather be dead in Clarksville than alive in Uvalde.

II

GETTING ON IN WEST TEXAS

II

Getting On in West Texas

*T*HE health-seeker tried life in Uvalde, however, and had the good luck to make a favorable impression on Judge John H. Clark, the leading lawyer of the place. Judge Clark was nearly twice Garner's age. He was looking for a younger man to make the rounds of surrounding country courts, which might mean a ride of two hundred miles.

23

John Garner got a trial. His performance was satisfactory and in the fullness of time Judge Clark took the newcomer into his firm, changing the sign to read Clark, Fuller & Garner.

John was proud of that sign. He strolled down Getty Street to Sewell and Estes' saloon, a sort of civic center, to be on hand in case he should be singled out for congratulations on his step up in the profession. Sure enough, a patron of Sewell and Estes' had noticed the new shingle: Clark, Fuller & Garner.

"Clark's fuller 'n Garner," he announced to the assembled company. "Boys, that ought to call for one on the junior member."

The junior member would have been the last man in town to dispute that.

John Garner had much to learn. Coming from Red River County to Uvalde he had travelled five hundred miles and in some respects had seen the calendar roll back a couple of generations. Indian wars were just over in East Texas when Rebecca Garner got there. Indian wars were a living memory in the Rio Grande country when John got there. The Red River country was

24

backwoods South, the Rio Grande cow-country West. One had to adjust oneself to new and unusual standards of value—to hearing forty thousand acres spoken of with the ease a quarter section would be mentioned on Blossom Prairie. A ride of twenty miles might be a trip to the post office.

The trade of a lawyer has much to do with the machinery of government. In theory this machinery was the same in West Texas as East. The same statutes applied, administered by the same devices. That was the theory; the practice was something else, and this practice had grown out of necessity, convenience and the power the strong are able quickly to arrogate to themselves in a frontier society. The great ranchmen were princes and their ranches principalities: the King Ranch contained one million two hundred and fifty thousand acres and the Kenedy Ranch, four hundred thousand acres. Old Captain King and old Captain Kenedy had come into that country as partners, carrying their law along with them and spreading it over vast domains. Every man in his own sphere, large or small, was

a lesser King or Kenedy in that he carried with
him a bit of law, as likely as not taking the form
of a cedar-handled, single-action Colt .45.

When John Garner left home his father had
said to him: "Tell the truth and try to be a
gentleman." John will say for himself that he has
always told the truth, and no one questions it. In
business, in politics or any other intercourse the
man who has John Garner's word for something
has a good deal. This was an asset for a young
man starting out in West Texas which to this
day is not a whole lot given to written instruments of contract. When Garner first went there
he saw deals running into thousands of dollars
made without either party leaving his saddle and
carried to conclusion over periods of months or
years without a scratch of a pen. It was not much
of a field for a comma-in-the-wrong-place petti-
fogger.

On horseback or by buckboard John Garner
attended courts in nine counties. On the way
from one to another if he could not make a ranch
house at night he would roll up in a blanket on
the ground beside the road. Cases dealt mostly

with horse and cow theft and with land—cloudy
titles and hazy boundaries. Some of the county
seats he visited consisted of a court house, a
couple of saloons and four or five other buildings.
Garner learned the art of settling cases outside
the court house. He would get litigants and
opposing counsel together over a friendly glass
and save the time, expense and trouble of a trial.
In this kind of negotiation John Garner became
increasingly skilful and he acquired the basis of a
useful acquaintance over a big stretch of country.

To begin with, Garner's share in the firm's fees
was one-sixth, which the first year brought him
between five hundred and six hundred dollars.
Cash was scarce and the lawyers accepted cattle,
goats, wool, hogs and saddle horses in exchange
for their services. For reorganizing a bank they
would get a slice of bank stock; for assisting a
rancher out of his troubles a slice of land. To
convert livestock into assets more conveniently
carried had been a considerable problem until
John Garner joined the firm. He proved a born
trader who sometimes would triple a fee in value.
This was an improvement over the day when the

27

firm had been accustomed to disposing of its chattel fees at a discount.

Judge Clark boosted the junior partner's share of the firm's take. Presently Mr. Garner's professional income was running around fifteen hundred to two thousand a year, which was a lot for a lawyer in that time and place and which John supplemented by playing poker. He lived frugally, invested in mortgages and began buying into an abstract company.

In the spring of 1895 the county judgeship of Uvalde fell vacant and John N. Garner announced his candidacy for the appointment to fill the unexpired term. In a little better than three years the tenderfoot from Red River had made himself enough of a West Texan to have the announcement considered seriously. Opposition came from an unexpected quarter, however.

Mariette Elizabeth Rheiner was not then and never became a votes-for-women advocate and, on the whole, she believes a woman better off in a home than meddling in public affairs. Besides, in 1895 she was not old enough to vote. Yet people listened—for amusement, at any rate—to

28

what Miss Etty had to say on the subject of the judgeship. She was a bright and a pretty girl; the orphaned daughter of old Peter Rheiner, the ranchman; and she'd been east to college. Miss Etty contended that Lawyer Garner's reputed exploits at the poker table did not constitute the proper qualifications for the bench.

But there was a miscarriage of justice and John Garner got the appointment. A little later Miss Etty was on a train to San Antonio when someone touched her arm.

"May I present Judge Garner?" said the introducer, emphasizing the title.

The twenty-six-year-old jurist set out to disarm his good-looking adversary. He succeeded so well that five months later he married Etty Rheiner.

Uvalde thought that Judge Garner had done well in the matter of matrimony. Mariette's father, Peter John Rheiner, an educated Swiss speaking German, French, Italian and Spanish, had made a long-distance rush to the California gold fields in the Fifties. In Louisiana in 1861 he had joined the Confederate Army. Penniless

29

and suffering from wounds in 1865, he had drifted to West Texas. In infancy Mariette lost her mother and grew up with three half-brothers born after her father's second marriage. On the forty-thousand-acre ranch in Uvalde County the family spoke German and Spanish as much as it did English. Mr. Rheiner built a school for his children and those of neighboring ranchers and brought a schoolmaster from New England.

When Mariette was twelve her father died, leaving her a fifth interest in the family property. The girl went to San Antonio to school and to Tennessee to college. Returning to Uvalde she found life so dull that she followed a girl friend to San Antonio and enrolled with her in a secretarial school merely for something to do. Shorthand was not an indispensible commodity in Uvalde, so Etty did not try to use it. She divided her time between home and southern cities such as New Orleans, Nashville and Atlanta where she had schoolmates.

Thus frontier life and the society of drawing rooms were known alike by Miss Etty. As a child she remembered her father's absences from the ranch. He would return from San Antonio with a load of provisions, his gold stowed in a hollow plank that was part of the wagon bed. Ranch-house windows were provided with shutters that would turn a rifle ball and the walls were loop-holed to resist attack. Peter Rheiner's Spanish-speaking cowboys kept close to the house when the boss was away. Once or twice roving Indians rode near but did not attack. Though the frontier was home to Etty she liked drawing-room life, too, and her absences from Uvalde were getting longer when by chance she returned in time to involve herself in the county judgeship contest.

John Garner spent four years on the bench and out of office hours he nursed his private investments. They thrived, for the Judge was still a good trader. In 1899 he went to the Texas Legislature. In the sophisticated city of Austin the new lawgiver laid aside his broad West Texas hat and bought a derby, which proved one of the few poor investments John Garner ever made. Mrs. Garner teased him so that he did not wear it very long.

Mrs. Garner had brushed up on her shorthand and gone along to Austin on the theory that she could be useful as her husband's secretary. Though a desire to mingle in the social life of the Texas capital may have been a contributing factor, Mrs. Garner's main hypothesis was sound. She made a useful secretary. Moreover she served a rather thrilling apprenticeship in the business of government. She had a part in the rise of her husband, in two terms, from an obscure representative from the West, unknown outside a string of half-empty counties along the Rio Grande, to something of a power in the Texas Legislature. There used to be a saying about West Texas to the effect that one could see farther and see less than anywhere else in the Union, there being nothing to obstruct the view. In four years' time John Garner projected himself upon that vacant sky line so high that when shooting off his fireworks one could spot him from one end of Texas to the other. He was elected to a second term without opposition, and on his retirement in 1902 he was an acknowledged spokesman for West Texas from Brownsville at the

THE COUNTY JUDGE OF UVALDE: MR. GARNER IN 1895

mouth of the Rio Grande to the Oklahoma line of the Panhandle, a thousand miles away.

This is not to imply that Representative Garner was uniformly victorious in the causes he espoused, or that he deserved to be. He lost plenty of fights, conspicuous ones. He lost a fight during his first week in Austin when he plunged, too impulsively for a greenhorn member, into the speakership contest. But Garner could lose a fight without sulking and he could win one without giving umbrage to the opposition.

During his first term Garner got a name for being death on pork-barrel bills. He was a member of the judiciary committee which the papers christened the "Bluebeard Committee" for its murderous work on money-spending legislation. Of two hundred bills to go before that body only four were reported out with favorable recommendations. Garner lost a fight for a convention to revise the outgrown state constitution written fifty-four years before by statesmen who had lately been citizens of the Texas Republic. He lost the first rounds of his fight to require insurance companies to invest a part of their

33

premium returns in Texas and to curb the rapacity of railroads which maintained a well-oiled and well-heeled lobby in Austin. When speaking of out-of-state corporations some of Representative Garner's remarks on the floor sounded pretty savage. The long-standing feuds between the ranching interests on the one hand and the agricultural and industrial interests on the other he handled more adroitly, doing most of his talking in committees. In the same discreet way he adjusted differences touching the conflicting interests of the large and the small ranch owners— which was at once good legislative and good political tactics.

The United States census figures for 1900 interested the gentleman from Uvalde profoundly. They showed West Texas entitled to another congressman. In due course a redistricting committee of the legislature was formed to attend to the matter. On this committee appeared the name of John N. Garner, who had an object in view. He had lifted his eyes to the hills and wanted to go to Washington.

III

THE CONGRESSMAN FROM THE RIO GRANDE

III

The Congressman from the Rio Grande

$\mathcal{T}$HE existing congressional district along the Rio Grande was an empire as to size. John Garner got it split in two. Uvalde was allocated to the new Fifteenth District which by no accident included the other counties that Attorney Garner had toured as the itinerant member of the firm of Clark, Fuller & Garner, cultivating acquaintances among the leading politicians. The district, when John got through whittling it out, was no pocket borough, however. Embracing a hundred-and-fifty-mile sweep of coast line and four hundred crow-flight miles along the Rio Grande, from the mouth to the Big Bend country, in all it shaped up about as big as Pennsylvania. But the people were farther apart, there being altogether about a hundred and sixty thousand; and along a good deal of the border eight out of ten of those spoke only Spanish. John had learned enough Spanish to pass the time of day with his Latin constituents; and he could cuss very satisfactorily in that tongue.

Having got his district on the map the next step was to get the Democratic nomination for congressman. For this there existed, in 1902, a regular formula in West Texas.

Half of the twenty-two counties in the new district being without a railroad, or other roads that were better than cattle trails, such centralization of affairs as obtained was in the hands of a few men of property and influence, for example: Archie Parr of Duval County, locally known as

the Free State of Duval; James B. Wells of
Brownsville, attorney for the King and the Kenedy ranches; Judge John Valls of Laredo; Robert
J. Kleberg of Kingsville, manager of the King
Ranch and son-in-law of its founder; Manuel
Guerra of Starr County; Tom Coleman of Dim-
mitt; Pat F. Dunn of Nueces, rancher and princi-
pal owner of Padre Island which stretches about
one hundred and fifteen miles along the coast,
from Corpus Christi Bay to the Rio Grande. The
way to get a nomination was to know enough men
like these. John Garner knew a sufficient number
to get the nomination without opposition at the
district convention at Laredo, after which the
delegates fired off anvils by way of relaxation
from their labors.

The next step was a state convention to ratify
district nominations, frame a state ticket and
adopt a platform. In 1902 the state convention
was held in Galveston. In the crowd milling
about the lobby of the Tremont House someone
dragged before Pat Dunn a small, red-faced,
sandy-haired man in a seersucker suit damp
with perspiration. Curiously, the rancher from

39

Corpus Christi and the ex-legislator from Uvalde had never met before.

"Mr. Dunn, I want you to know John Garner."

"I didn't catch the name," said Dunn.

"John Garner is the name," volunteered the small man. "Your nominee for Congress."

Dunn backed off to get a better perspective on the figure before him. "Well, by God," he exclaimed. "Hereafter I want to see 'em first."

Dunn had directed the Nueces County delegation to support John Garner simply on the say-so of his fellow-ranchman, Robert Kleberg, and Kleberg's attorney, Judge Wells of Brownsville.

In Congress Garner proved to be better than he looked. He put on no airs, he franked no long-winded speeches home, in fact he made no speeches. The truth is in 1903 there was little a new Democratic congressman could do except to keep his eyes open and his mouth shut, observing and learning. Now and then a chance would present itself to strike a lick for the home district by snatching an appropriation crumb from the Republican table. For instance, that vast pork-barrel omnibus, the Rivers and Harbors Bill,

included a modest sum for deepening the water-
way at Corpus Christi. A board of Army engineers
reported adversely on the project, whereupon it
was stricken out. Roy Miller, editor of the Corpus
Christi *Caller* and president of the Commercial
Club, journeyed to Washington to see what could
be done. It seemed that nothing could be done.
The Army had spoken and the Republican majority on the Rivers and Harbors Committee was
not in a mood to concern itself further in the
matter.

Roy was young, filled with ambition and learning the ropes in Washington. He saw Garner and
Garner went to work. He got on the good side of
old General Marshall, the chief of engineers.
The General was as fat as his chief, Secretary of
War Taft, and within six weeks of retirement for
age.

"Garner, you're right," said the General after
the Representative from Uvalde had presented
his case. "It's time I showed those young squirts
who's boss. I'll overrule the board and recom-
mend the improvement of the Corpus Christi
harbor."

41

Armed with General Marshall's veto Garner got a subcommittee to vote to restore the item. But by the time this was done the Rivers and Harbors Committee was to report its bill on the morning of the following day. The committee would act only on printed amendments. Late in the afternoon Garner went to the public printer and asked him to put the amendment in type over night. The printer refused. He was burdened with work that had to be done by morning. Garner's persuasive eloquence was in vain. No one but the Speaker of the House could order that amendment in type over night.

The Speaker was Joseph G. Cannon, famed for his autocratic and partisan rule.

"I'll see Cannon," Garner said to Miller.

Miller called one of Washington's rare taxis and took Garner to the Speaker's residence on Vermont Avenue. Garner went inside and the Texas editor waited—two hours, while the taxi meter clicked and Miller grew anxious because his expense allowance was not very large.

When Garner came out he had his amendment

with a pencilled notation in the Speaker's hand to put it in print.

"How in the world did you do it?" asked the admiring Miller.

"I sometimes play in the Speaker's poker game," remarked Garner.

The Corpus Christi item went in the bill and the bill went through.

That is a fair sample of John Garner's early work and one reason he did not have to make speeches or to insert unmade ones in the *Congressional Record* to impress the people at home. Nothing in the public records bore witness to Garner's connection with the landing of the Corpus Christi appropriation. The Congressman from the Fifteenth Texas District was not a member of the Rivers and Harbors Committee. But the people in Southwest Texas knew Garner had done the work, and that was what counted with the voters. It solidified Garner's strength at home and gave him a little firmer hold on his job while affording time and opportunity to study the Washington picture and learn the rudiments of the trade of national lawmaking. It relieved him of the necessity of constantly seeking the limelight for home consumption—and that is an important thing.

John Garner had risen fast in the Texas Legislature. Many an inexperienced congressman would have expected to do the same in Washington—a feat which was not possible for a Democrat in 1903. In this situation many a congressman would have felt that he had to put on a show anyhow and would have wasted a lot of time trying to make himself conspicuous in the eyes of the people at home. It is possible for a congressman to perpetuate himself in office for quite a long time merely by playing to the home galleries. Such congressmen are worthless as national legislators; the important men in the House regard them as unmitigated nuisances. Garner did not fall into this too-common error though it must have hurt him a little to become a Nobody in Washington after having been Somebody in West Texas.

By the time they came to Washington Mr. and Mrs. Garner were well-to-do, but did not show it in their style of living at the capital. As they were strangers to the city Mr. Garner had registered at the Normandie Hotel on arriving, a pleasant old place and the Washington residence of Senator Charles A. Culbertson of Texas. But the Garners regarded it as too expensive and they found themselves one of the typical Washington boarding houses of the period, run by Mrs. Lillie B. Creel List in K Street just across from Franklin Park. The park was a fine playground for the Garners' only child, Tully. Tully was seven and had been named for Tully Fuller of the law firm of Clark, Fuller & Garner. Excepting committee chairmen, congressmen were not provided with offices at that time. Mr. Garner did his work in a room at the boarding house, his wife acting as his secretary. They stayed at Mrs. List's for three years.

In those days the organization of the House was almost purely a matter for the Speaker, acting for a closed corporation of majority leaders. Mr. Cannon designated committee assignments of the Republican members and named committee chairmen. The unknown from West Texas fared more poorly than usual in the assignment shuffle. He was given the last place on the minority side of two minor committees—Railways and Canals and Expenditures in the State Department.

But before Mr. Garner had an opportunity to learn, if so disposed, the business before the committees on which he had been designated to serve, he must take a stand on the Cuban Reciprocity Bill. President Theodore Roosevelt had called the Congress in special session, a month before the regular session should begin, to dispose of this pet measure of his. It virtually provided for free trade between Cuba and the United States. The country was for it and a Democratic congressional caucus voted to support the President. John Garner said nothing in the caucus, but he told his friends on the Texas delegation that he intended to vote against the bill, which in his opinion favored commercial interests of the North and East over the South and West. Ten days after Congress had convened the House voted. The bill was passed three hundred and fifty-six to twenty-one. Among the twenty-one was Representative Garner, the only Texan in the House, with one exception, to oppose the bill.

During his first term Garner himself introduced a few small bills: for a public building at Eagle Pass, Texas; to pension a widow; to survey the channel at Aransas Pass, on the Gulf coast; to construct a coast-wise canal in Texas; to establish a weather bureau at Del Rio, Texas; to enlarge the personnel of the United States Court of Claims which was chronically behind in its work. All but the last-named were little local measures by which congressmen seek to keep on the good side of their constituents. The noteworthy thing is not that Garner introduced such bills but that he introduced so few of them. Considering the size of his district, and the thousands of similar bills that go into the legislative hopper at each session, the average of the young man from Uvalde was low.

At committee meetings, where the real work of Congress is done, the Texan was punctual, inquiring and diligent. Before the session was over he was well-informed for a first-termer and well-liked personally by his committee colleagues.

47

The long vacations between sessions Mr. Garner spent at home casually but shrewdly inspecting his political fences and looking after his prospering private investments. In 1904 he was re-elected.

The time was to come when John N. Garner would evoke comparison with Henry Clay for the dexterity with which he handled the affairs of the House from the Speaker's dais. In 1904, however, it was not foreseen that Mr. Garner should become Speaker of the House. Any comparison with the statesman from Kentucky would have rested on their mutual fondness for draw poker.

Mr. Clay, Daniel Webster and Sam Houston were leading lights of the first Washington poker game to achieve national renown. Down the political generations to the present day the capital has seldom been without its poker game involving some of our public life's most distinguished figures. In this respect John Garner had come to Washington equipped to stand with the best. The important game to get in was one presided over by Uncle Joe Cannon at a celebrated

THE CONGRESSMAN FROM THE RIO GRANDE: MR. GARNER IN 1908

hideaway in K Street known as the Boar's Nest. Incidentally the Boar's Nest turned out to be quite a hothouse for Vice-Presidents. Besides the droll young Texan with his leathery face and cow-country squint two regulars at Uncle Joe's round table were Representative "Sunny Jim" Sherman of New York and Senator Charley Curtis of Kansas.

Not all the profit John Garner took away from that table was in return for blue chips. Speaker Cannon admired a good poker player and the admiration of the autocrat of the House was a helpful thing to have. One evening Uncle Joe said:

"Garner, where is your seat on the floor?"

In those days representatives occupied designated seats as senators still do. The question was an important one for Mr. Garner because a discriminating use of the power of recognition ranked high among the devices comprising the bag of parliamentary tricks by which old Uncle Joe ruled the House.

Garner sought to take no undue advantage of the privilege implied by the Speaker's inquiry, which was another thing Mr. Cannon appreciated. Not long afterward the Texan received his reward.

February 25, 1905, was set aside for the reception by Congress, for Statuary Hall in the Capitol, of likenesses in marble of Stephen F. Austin and Sam Houston. Several Texas representatives prepared orations extolling the virtues of those heroes. Mr. Cannon canvassed the situation. Learning that John Garner intended to make no speech, when the House convened the Speaker said:

"The gentleman from Texas, Mr. Garner, will please take the chair."

There were members of the House who had never heard of John N. Garner, even by name, until that moment.

Mr. Garner discharged his duties with a minimum of words, recognizing one after another his more articulate colleagues in the order agreed upon.

Not until more than a year later did Garner make his first speech from the floor. Representative John M. Pinckney, of Texas, an advocate of prohibition, had been shot to death while addressing an anti-saloon rally in Texas. Mr. Garner was not a prohibitionist. He rose, however, to pay a brief tribute to one who had believed differently from him and who had given his life in defense of his principles.

During the same session Mr. Garner offered a bill on the unanimous consent calendar to provide that the Federal district and circuit courts hold sessions at Del Rio, Texas, in his district. Cagey old Sereno E. Payne, the Republican leader, rose to ask:

"Is there any public building lurking around this bill anywhere?"

"I will say to the gentleman from New York that there is not just at this time," replied Garner. "The people from this district have to travel from one hundred to four hundred and twenty miles to get to court. The bill would shorten the distance for them from thirty-five to two hundred and fifty miles."

It went on the calendar and was passed. Next session Representative Garner got his courthouse building.

Shortly after the exchange with Payne the

Texan raised a point on the floor which touched one of the sources of the Speaker's power. He asked that bills on the calendar be considered in the order they had been reported by committees rather than at the discretion of the Speaker. Twice he insisted on this point and, in the matter in question, won it. The incident carried Mr. Garner into an interesting current of action which was beginning to manifest itself in the affairs of the House: for not Democrats only were wearying of the dictatorship by which Speaker Cannon and a small group of hardshell Republicans controlled the program of the House of Representatives.

In the closing weeks of his first term Mr. Garner did something else of more than passing interest, in the light of later events. He introduced a bill to provide for a tax on the gross incomes of all persons and corporations in the United States, graduated as follows:

> Annual incomes under $1000 one one-
>   hundredth of 1 percent
> Annual incomes $1000 to $10,000 one-
>   half of 1 percent

Annual incomes $10,000 to $100,000 1
  percent
Annual incomes above $100,000 5 per-
  cent

This was one of the first graduated income-tax
bills introduced in an American congress. Referred to the Committee on Ways and Means it
was ordered printed. There was no further consideration. When the session ended Mr. Garner's
income-tax bill died in the files of that committee,
along with a cartload of other measures. That
happens at the close of every session. Not one
in a hundred of those bills is ever heard of again,
except possibly by way of electioneering in the
introducer's home district. It is unlikely that
John Garner introduced this bill for local campaign purposes, the cattle barons on the Rio
Grande, no less than the barons of Wall Street
and of Pittsburgh, believing taxes numerous
enough already.

Mr. Garner's idea of a graduated income tax
had a long sleep, but it did not die.

IV

A CONGRESSMAN COMES OF AGE

IV

A Congressman Comes of Age

UNCLE JOE CANNON used the Boar's Nest as a laboratory for the study of men as well as a means of recreation. The Speaker had come to Congress in 1873. There was little about the complicated mechanics of legislation he did not know; and to suit his own and his party's purposes he moved men, including some of the Democrats, as a chess player moves his pieces.

MR. GARNER OF TEXAS

In a much lesser way Mr. Garner of Texas was able to put the Speaker's poker club to the same uses. There in a comparatively short while he familiarized himself with some of the characteristics of key men in the House which he might have been years learning under more formal conditions. The Texan was a good fellow, a tolerably good mixer—not too forward and not too reserved. Meeting President Roosevelt, Garner began to talk about hunting along the Rio Grande. T. R. asked fifty questions and the two men got along fine. The acquaintance between the President and the young border Congressman grew with the years. Garner used to take hunter friends to the White House and Mr. Roosevelt followed Garner's recommendation in naming a postmaster of Uvalde.

This camaraderie, this faculty for having something to say to everyone he meets, particularly those in the opposite political camp, will not make a man an influential figure in Congress, but it will help. Assigned to the Committee on Foreign Affairs, Garner made the acquaintance of pleasure-loving and able young Nicholas Longworth, who also had entered Congress in 1903. On the surface two more dissimilar men than the cultivated, aristocratic Longworth and the homespun Texan would have been hard to find in the House. Yet a friendship resulted which was to last the lifetime of Mr. Longworth and to make much House history.

Other House history was nearer to hand, however. Representative George W. Norris of Nebraska had begun his service in the House on the day that Garner did. Like Garner he had been a local judge. Like Garner he chafed under the dictatorial sway of Mr. Cannon over the House but, unlike Garner, Norris's discomfiture did not bear the stamp of partisan interest, for the Nebraskan was a Republican. Norris wrote a resolution calling for a modernization of the House rules and he carried it in his pocket until it became dogeared. In the upper house a La Follette-led revolt against the leadership of Senator Aldrich, who ruled that chamber about as Cannon did the House, succeeded, and Norris waited his chance. This came when in March, 1910, Cannon incautiously moved to abolish "Calendar Wednesday." Calendar Wednesday represented a mild relaxation of the grip the Speaker held on the House. On that day members could obtain, or attempt to obtain, action on bills which Cannon's hand-picked committees had suppressed.

The Speaker's tactically inept move brought a roar of disapproval from liberal Republicans. Norris plumped in his resolution which called for the taking of the Committee on Rules out of the Speaker's hands. This committee had five members. The Speaker was chairman and the majority members were his personal appointees. The Norris resolution called for a committee of fifteen members, elected by the House.

The insurgent Victor Murdock, a Kansas editor whom Cannon had lately demoted in committee ranking as a disciplinary measure, rallied the liberal Republicans and began working on the waverers. The Democratic leader, Champ Clark, moved into the fray, designating the personable member from Uvalde to lend the Murdock group any discreet aid in his power. It was a ticklish assignment. Too much pressure or pressure clumsily exerted from the Democratic side would have antagonized the Republicans who were on the fence. For twenty-nine hours the debate raged, which was all very well for the public but speeches in Congress change few votes. While the orators filled the newspaper columns with their remarks Garner worked in the cloakrooms. He was by no means responsible for the result that followed but he had enough of a hand in it to win the favorable opinion of Champ Clark. By a vote of 191 to 156 the Norris resolution was adopted. The Republican old guard roundly beaten, Mr. Taft's administration was headed downhill.

That autumn John Garner was re-elected to serve his fifth term. The important election news, however, was that the Democrats, for the first time in sixteen years, would control the next House of Representatives. But there was still the lame-duck session of the old House with Mr. Cannon in the chair and the Republicans in control—a control somewhat modified, however, by the ire of the insurgents against the standpatters. In the last days of this session the Republicans resorted to the usual tactics of a party about to yield its ascendency. Jokers in appropriation and other routine bills concealed efforts to "freeze" Republicans in office, to perpetuate party advantages and leave the Democrats as little clover as possible. Combatting these efforts John Garner for the first time in his life became a real factor in the House debates. Demonstrating a wide knowledge of legislative processes, of governmental machinery, of the rules of the House, of the procedure of committees and of the innumerable items that make up the supply bills, he proved that his eight silent years had been spent in profitable observation.

On March 5, 1911, Champ Clark was elected Speaker and on April 24 he took the chair at a special session of the new Congress. On the same day Mr. Garner was on his feet opposing a Democratic resolution to create certain extra clerkships at six dollars a day to supplant regular clerkships at one hundred and twenty-five dollars a month. Out of his minute familiarity with the internal administration of the business of the House and of its committees, Garner showed these extra jobs simply to be attempts at pay-roll padding. Certainly, that is what they were; but the practice had the sanction of long usage, and the House Democrats had been away from the patronage trough for sixteen long years.

A few days later the economical Texan interrupted his colleagues to object to the appointment of an additional clerk for the Committee on Territories. He said that the Democrats had been criticizing the Republicans for extravagance and the Republicans had been able to get along without this extra clerk. Nor was that all. Within the next few weeks Garner had demanded that the expenses of the Sugar Trust investigating committee go through the regular Committee on Accounts; opposed the payment of cab fare to representatives serving on special committees who had to come to the Capitol anyhow; opposed the payment of witness fees to government employes appearing before such committees; challenged an item of eight hundred dollars for editing the *Congressional Directory* when he learned that the newspaperman who did the work farmed it out to an employe of the Government Printing Office for two hundred and fifty dollars;

63

objected to granting certain employes of Congress a month's extra pay presumably in lieu of expenses home between sessions.

Later a bill came in to appropriate seven thousand dollars to defray the expenses of eight senators and twelve representatives to go to St. Louis to dedicate the Jefferson memorial. Mr. Garner suggested that this amounted to three hundred and fifty dollars a member for travelling expenses to and from St. Louis, with one day in that city. Tom Heflin of Alabama was in charge of the bill. He opened his defense of it with an eloquent tribute to Thomas Jefferson as the father of American democracy. He concluded by saying that while he, personally, had not checked the details of the anticipated expenditures, other members had checked them and he felt that the House could have every confidence in their judgment.

Mr. Garner's rejoinder was brief.

"I have no confidence in anybody," said he, "who figures that it will cost three hundred and fifty dollars for a man to go to St. Louis for one day."

MARIETTE RHEINER GARNER IN 1908

These tactics by Garner irritated some deserving Democrats, but Speaker Clark and the party leaders who controlled the House program were satisfied. The Texan advertised the Democrats as the taxpayers' friends. Gradually more responsible work was found for Garner. Clark made him a member of the conference committee to iron out differences of opinion with reference to the Diplomatic and Consular Bill. A conference committee is a joint body of senators and representatives. Such an assignment carries a certain distinction, especially where, as in this instance, the Senate is controlled by the opposite party.

In 1912 the Democrats won the Senate and the presidency as well. With all the patronage of the Federal government at their command they were in clover for fair and John Garner was busier than ever trying to see that they did not founder themselves.

The most important committee of the House is that of Ways and Means. Money-raising legislation originates in the House and the Committee on Ways and Means is the bottleneck through which it must pass to get action on the floor. Membership on this committee is eagerly sought. With it goes much responsibility and much labor. Members are carefully chosen both by the party in power and by the opposition. A slipshod or incompetent majority on the Committee on Ways and Means can do much damage to an administration. A careful and alert minority can enhance the fortunes of the party out of power.

When the House organized in 1913 John N. Garner asked for assignment to the Committee on Ways and Means. He was not the only candidate for membership in that body, and it was clear that many of the aspirants must be disappointed. Garner was asked to withdraw his bid. The chairmanship of the Committee on Foreign Affairs, on which Garner had advanced near the top by seniority, was held out to him. Garner said he wished to retire from the Committee on Foreign Affairs. Its work was not his forte. That of the Committee on Ways and Means was. More persuasions ensued, and failed. The question of Ways and Means membership was thrown into a caucus of the Democratic members. John N.

Garner of Texas received the highest number of votes given anyone on the list of candidates.

Coming to the committee with unusual equipment for a new member, Garner had an important if unspectacular role in the framing of the Underwood Tariff Bill, named for Oscar Underwood, chairman of the Ways and Means Committee. Mr. Garner's chief contribution was the income-tax provision in that bill.

The first income tax, during the Civil War, was a flat three-percent levy on gross incomes over eight hundred dollars, with no deductions except for taxes paid. After Appomattox it was dropped. In 1870 a flat levy of two and one-half percent was laid for one year. In 1894 the Democrats included in their tariff bill a provision for a two-percent tax on incomes over four thousand dollars. The act was thrown out by the Supreme Court, in a five to four decision reversing previous decisions of the court, one justice going so far as to call an income tax class legislation and an "assault on capital." The Democrats continued to call it as just a tax as could be laid, a feature which Garner tried to carry further by regulating the amount of the tax according to capacity to pay. Incidentally his 1905 bill had contained a provision aimed at getting around the constitutional objection raised by the Supreme Court majority in its decision invalidating the 1894 tax. But the Democratic leadership had chosen to try to amend the Constitution expressly legitimatizing the income tax. After a long struggle this had been accomplished in 1913.

Garner at once contended for a graduated tax. He was opposed by Chairman Underwood and such influential Democratic colleagues, later to distinguish themselves in the Wilson administration, as A. Mitchell Palmer, Francis Burton Harrison and Andrew Peters. They wanted a flat rate applying to rich and poor alike. Garner hammered away with his capacity-to-pay theory. He started backfires in the home states of his distinguished adversaries. He won and a scaled schedule ranging from one percent to six percent, according to the size of the income, was adopted. This was the beginning of the modern income-tax system in the United States.

When Mr. Underwood went to the Senate

A CONGRESSMAN COMES OF AGE

Claude Kitchen of North Carolina succeeded to the chairmanship of the Committee on Ways and Means. Mr. Kitchen and President Wilson did not get along well together. Speaker Clark nursed the wounds inflicted at the Baltimore Convention where Mr. Wilson had prevailed over the Missourian for the presidential nomination. The President found the breezy Texan easier to talk to than those leaders, and equally well-informed. Garner began to be included among the congressional notables called to the White House for consultation.

In April, 1917, Mr. Garner voted for the War Resolution. A few days later his son, Tully, who had finished college the year before, was in his father's office.

"Son," said Mr. Garner, "how do you feel about going to war?"

"I aim to go, Dad," said the boy.

"I'm glad to hear it—for you've got to go. I couldn't have cast that vote to send other fathers' boys to war if I hadn't known I was sending my own. And just one more thing: your mother and I will want to hear from you every time you get a chance to write, but promise you'll never ask me for a favor. I might be in a position to get it and I don't want to be exposed to the temptation."

During the ensuing two years Mr. Garner contributed nothing to the library of oratory about the "brave boys" who were serving their flag. Once he interrupted a speech on the floor to say it would be more to the point if a way could be arranged to have soldiers in hospitals paid promptly; again to make an inquiry about the facilities for getting mail to the troops in France; again to suggest that it would be a good thing if relatives could be notified more punctually when men were wounded.

All war financing started in the Committee on Ways and Means. Four Liberty loans, aggregating $17,975,451,950 were floated in addition to the after-the-Armistice Victory loan of $4,500,-000,000 and War Savings Certificates totalling about $900,000,000. Two sweeping emergency tax bills were adopted, one in 1917 and one in 1918. The speed with which the United States, starting from scratch, created a war machine, placed two million fighting men in France and supplied them is still a marvel to students of the military science. The policy was not to quibble too much about profits and thus delay production but to try to equalize things by putting the tax-gatherer's hand in the munition-maker's pocket afterward. Excess profits taxes ran as high as seventy-five percent.

Near the end of the debate on the Revenue Bill of 1918 Representative J. Hampton Moore, a Republican of Pennsylvania, said on the floor:

"I wish to pay a public tribute to the gentleman from Texas. He seldom makes a speech on this floor and thus denies the public the benefit of his wisdom, but in committee he is so adroit and skilful a legislator that few can equal him."

At another time when a member complimented Mr. Garner for his committee work the Texan said it would be unfair not to extend the praise to include the Republican members of the Ways and Means Committee.

These tremendous activities brought a need for constant and confidential liaison between the House of Representatives and the Executive

Mansion. Postmaster General Burleson, himself a Texan, suggested to Mr. Wilson that Garner would be the man for this. Mr. Wilson sent for Garner. Finding him thoroughly versed in the business of the House, quick with sensible suggestions and no waster of words, the President asked Garner to come to the White House twice a week at five in the evening. Throughout the War this schedule was adhered to as nearly as the President's appointments would permit. Not five members of the House knew of the arrangement, and few in the Executive establishment aside from Joseph P. Tumulty, the President's private secretary, and Secretary of the Treasury McAdoo appear to have known of it. Mr. Garner would ride from Capitol Hill in a street car and enter the private secretary's office. If the newspapermen spotted him he would say he wanted to see Joe Tumulty. Then he would pass through the corridor from the executive offices to the President's private study on the second floor of the White House proper. Leaving, he would pass through Tumulty's office again.

Some of the discussions with the President

were very candid. Particularly, it took a lot of convincing to get Garner's assent to the policy of huge loans to the Allies. One time the Texan found himself leaning over and pounding the President's knee for emphasis.

His face redder than it usually is, the congressional envoy straightened up and apologized. Mr. Wilson only laughed.

Often Garner found the President pitifully weary. The visitor would try to cheer him up with a story. Mr. Wilson liked a good story or a tart rejoinder. One evening the President's face was white with fatigue.

"Garner," he said, "if it were not for my faith in the old Presbyterian belief in predestination I don't think I could carry this burden much longer."

Mr. Garner pretended not to understand Mr. Wilson's allusion to predestination.

"Mr. President, I'm the same way," he said. "Having grown up in the Red River Valley with all those darkies I'm superstitious as hell myself."

For an instant Mr. Wilson looked very gravely at his caller, and Mr. Garner was afraid he had said the wrong thing. Then the President leaned back and laughed.

"Garner, I think our 'superstitions' will carry us both through."

Once a proposed presidential appointment came under review. Garner disagreed with the President so strongly that, years after the War, he told a friend that Mr. Wilson had given him "the worst dressing down" he had received since his entry into politics. Before he could find out whether the incident had impaired his relationship with the White House Mr. Garner was taken to a hospital for a small operation. The next morning a vase of flowers appeared at his bedside, with a note from the President saying to hurry and get well.

V

NEAR THE TOP IN THE HOUSE

V

Near the Top in the House

$\mathcal{J}$OR a congressman to enjoy a good reputation on Capitol Hill and a good reputation in the country at large may be two different things. The country forms its opinion of a congressman largely from what he says on the floor and, in these days, over the radio. The Hill also takes that into consideration, but the major factor, by far, is the performance of the congressman behind the scenes in committees and in conferences. Thus a congressman may have a good reputation in the country at large and an inferior one among his colleagues, or vice versa. It is, of course, possible for a congressman to have a good reputation both places, as most of the very top layer of them do.

John N. Garner emerged from the War in the top layer. Informed observers placed him among the first ten Democratic members of the House in usefulness. He was, however, unknown to the country. In Congress he still seldom spoke on the floor and out of Congress he shunned the chautauqua circuits and the lecture platforms. When he did address the House he had a way of keeping his remarks confidential among the members present.

The public printer sends each member a proof of his remarks, as caught by the stenographer, for correction before they go in the *Congressional Record*. This courtesy enables the speeches of so many statesmen to read better than they sounded. Perhaps the most celebrated debate on the floors of Congress was that between Webster and Hayne over states' rights in Jackson's Day. Three generations of school children, North and South, learned by heart some of the rounded periods of those orators. What they learned may not have been precisely what thrilled the galleries in 1830, for both Mr. Webster and Mr. Hayne spent three weeks revising their manuscripts before releasing them for print and posterity.

Another congressional courtesy called "extension of remarks" enables congressmen to fascinate readers of the *Congressional Record* with speeches never delivered. Not only do the files of the the *Record* contain no undelivered speeches by John Garner, but until sometime after the War it contains virtually no speeches by him. Receiving printer's proofs for revision Mr. Garner had a habit of revising his remarks by striking them out, or reducing them to a few sentences. Protests from Democratic colleagues, who wanted to know where Garner stood and what he had said, ultimately ended this self-effacing practice. When elected Vice-President Mr. Garner called aside Milton West, his successor to the seat of the Fifteenth Texas District.

"It was a good many years before any remarks of mine got in the *Record;* and I hope you won't make a damn' fool of yourself either."

In 1920 when the Harding landslide swept the Democrats from power Mr. Garner was re-elected to serve his tenth term. The new Congress was filled with new faces. Men were there who had been boys in grade school when John Garner had first come to Washington and established his little family in Mrs. List's boarding house. The Texan's climb to eminence in legislative circles had been no overnight affair: he was a veteran who knew the ropes.

At fifty-one Mr. Garner's thatch of ruddy hair had turned almost white, imparting a patriarchal appearance which a salty tongue and an informal manner did something to neutralize. Nearly all the newcomers to Congress were Republicans, some of whom soon learned that for advice on the things any green congressman should know, Mr. Garner was as good a man to go to as one of the Republican leaders. Among these leaders was Garner's close friend Nicholas Longworth. Nick would accuse Jack of trying to seduce novitiate

Photograph by Acme

Senator Charles L. McNary of Oregon, Republican Leader of the Upper House, Senator Carter Glass of Virginia and the Vice-President preparing to do the honors at the opening of the baseball season in the Capital.

Republicans whom the people had sent to Washington to "redeem the government from Democratic mismanagement." This was said in jest. Nick knew that a young Republican seeking enlightenment on such non-partisan matters as House regulations or committee complexities could get an honest and straight answer from John Garner.

Changes also had come to the southwestern corner of Texas which comprises the Fifteenth Congressional District. A picturesque frontier was retreating. Sun-baked little cattle-country county seats, no more than wide spots in the road when John Garner had discovered them as the travelling member of his old law firm, had blossomed into thriving and sightly towns. Oil and the cultivation of citrus fruits in the lower Rio Grande Valley were altering the character of the countryside. District boundaries were changed, and changed again. As the district shrank in size it gained in population, making the retention of the political control a congressman must have to perpetuate himself in office a more complex proposition than in the days of a few ruling impresarios along the border. When Mr. Garner ceased to represent the district on March 4, 1933, it contained four hundred thousand people as against one hundred sixty thousand in a larger area in 1902.

The King and the Kenedy ranches were still there, however, and still politically powerful, the King Ranch comprising the largest reach of land owned by a single family in the United States. Together these two properties occupy about ninety percent of the landscape in Kenedy County and the King Ranch covers in addition four-fifths of Kleberg County and spills over into three other counties. The influence of these ranches on public affairs has been counterbalanced, however, by the population boom which filled up the citrus fruit belt. Many, perhaps most, of the two hundred thousand fruit growers hailed from the Republican states of the Middle West. In the Twenties they were the victims of a land speculation craze and the subsequent collapse of fictitious values almost on a Florida scale. Such things always bring about political repercussions. Mr. Garner weathered them, enough of the newcomers retaining the Fifteenth District habit of voting for the old-timer from Uvalde to keep him in office with a minimum of apparent effort on his part, even in 1928 when Texas went for Hoover. In the thirty years he represented that district Mr. Garner does not appear to have made a dozen campaign speeches in his own behalf.

Nor did he trim his sails to accommodate every shift in the local political winds. Texas went dry but Mr. Garner stubbornly refused to alter his opposition to prohibition. One of his campaign addresses was interrupted by a querulous listener who wanted to know if, in addition to being a wet, it was also true that Mr. Garner played cards.

"Yes," said the Congressman. "Game in Room 5, Starr Hotel, directly after this meeting."

When the Ku Klux Klan mushroomed over the South and the Middle West, dominating local elections, some of the most conspicuous public figures in Texas became open proponents of the kluxer point of view. As the election of 1922 approached Garner was advised to lay low and keep quiet. He refused, openly denouncing the Klan as un-American. A fiery cross was burned on a hill behind Mr. Garner's home in Uvalde. He was re-nominated and re-elected.

Two years later there was a little revolt on the part of the wealthy because of their congressman's sponsorship of the inheritance tax and his opposition to fat income-tax reductions for large taxpayers. By this time Mr. Garner himself was one of the richest men in the district.

Back of his house Mr. Garner built a long barbecue pit with benches to seat maybe a hundred people. During his last decade in the House that was where he did his campaigning. Mr. Garner's friends do not like the word campaigning. They say Mr. Garner has not campaigned since the War—merely "kept in touch with the people of the district." Anyway, this is what has happened. During the congressional vacations he would fill his barbecue benches about once a month—oftener probably on an election year—and by rotating guests entertain most of the important people of the district. Mr. Garner told them, and told all who inquired, that he believes in representative government, of which his conception is embodied in the following:

"If you re-elect me I'll go up there and do the best I can for you as long as it is the best for the country as I see it. As to details you'll have to trust my judgment. Don't write or wire me to support some bill just because the word has been passed around to devil your congressman. Even if you have read the bill, which will be unlikely, you won't know what it will be like in the final form. I will know this and I will vote to do what I think is right—for the Fifteenth District and for the country."

As a result Mr. Garner has been largely exempt from the influence of the pressure groups.

Mr. Garner's wealth is variously estimated to be from five hundred thousand to two million dollars. A million is supposed to be about right. In speaking of his private fortune he always says "we," meaning himself and Mrs. Garner. Judge Garner had some money saved when he married, but not so much as his bride with her fifth interest in an estate valued at a hundred thousand dollars.

"We kept our money rolling," Mr. Garner says, meaning that they kept turning it over.

The Garners began married life in a four-room house. Every Saturday night before going to bed they would sit down by the oil lamp and go over their books seeing just what had happened to their money during the week. As their fortune grew these accountings were made once a month. Now they cast a balance the first of each year.

Mr. Garner made his money the thrifty, small-town way. Bonanzas—even the Texas bonanzas: oil, sulphur, citrus fruit—never tempted him. He has never owned a share of stock traded on the New York Exchange; and when he first came to Congress tips—good ones—were freely circulated by lobbyists. In his early days he speculated a little in wheat on the Chicago and in cotton on the New Orleans board of trade, but discontinued that when he got to Washington. Though John Garner likes money and gets a real pleasure out of making it—even now, when he has more than he knows what to do with—his worst enemy would not suggest the faintest con-

86

nection between that circumstance and his official conduct. Well-paid lectures have long been regarded as a legitimate perquisite of public men. A Cabinet officer can get a thousand dollars an appearance, and poor men are obliged to supplement their official salaries. Mr. Garner has never delivered a lecture for pay, and probably not more than three or four free ones. In 1938 he turned down an offer of fifteen hundred dollars weekly for one fifteen-minute radio appearance a week, with the statement that John Garner was not worth that much and the vice-presidency of the United States was not for sale.

Sam Rayburn, who succeded Mr. Garner as Democratic floor leader in the House, says John has seventy-five cents of every dollar he ever made—a statement the Vice-President would esteem a high compliment. Mr. Garner likes to make room for a joke about his frugality. When he handed a ten-dollar bill to Senator Barbour of New Jersey in payment of a wager on a ball game Mr. Barbour asked him to autograph it.

"I want to give my grandson a souvenir," he said.

"Then let me make you out a check for the amount," volunteered the loser.

Mr. Garner permitted the Associated Press to circulate this one. The Vice-President had his shoes shined in the Union Station at St. Louis while stopping between trains. He gave a quarter to the colored boy who, having a touch of thrift himself, pocketed the coin with an expansive smile of thanks.

"See here," said the VP, "don't I get any change?"

"How much change you want, Cap'n?" asked the boy.

"A dime," said Mr. Garner.

For forty-five years Mr. Garner has had a considerable share of his fortune in personal loans, largely to people in and around Uvalde. For years at a time these loans have aggregated as much as a quarter of a million dollars. Yet not until 1938 did he sue a man who owed him. Then an agreed judgment was obtained in a friendly action to clear a land title. These remarks refer to personal loans by Mr. Garner, not loans by banks he owns or has stock in. Residents of

Uvalde tell many stories, however, of Mr. Garner's intercession with banks to prevent foreclosure on debtors. "Carry that man; I know he's good." Yet there have been occasions when bank examiners have thought differently and would not permit Mr. Garner's own banks to carry a debtor further. They had to collect the loan or write it off. In some such instances Mr. Garner has paid the bank, assuming the obligations himself. His losses, if any, have been small.

Mr. Garner believes people should pay their debts. This belief is one of the foundation stones of his not-very-elaborate economic and social theories. He says it builds character. His son Tully got his banking experience in the banks Mr. Garner controls. Someday Tully will own these properties. A few years ago, when ready for promotion to the management of one of them, the young man said he preferred to branch out on his own. He went to Amarillo and acquired control of the First National Bank there. To do this he needed more cash than he had at the time, and his father loaned him a considerable sum at eight percent, the legal rate in Texas. Soon after Tully found he could get money for six percent and told his father he would like to discharge the eight-percent notes.

"You can discharge them at maturity," said Mr. Garner. "The first thing a banker should learn is to fulfill a contract he has made."

The liquidation of chattels received as fees by his law firm familiarized John Garner with the profit-taking possibilities of about everything that can be bought, sold or swapped in West Texas. The list is not a long one. As a general thing Garner learned that any useful commodity that has dropped below the cost of production is a good buy provided one is in a position to carry it until the price comes back, as it always does eventually.

A hard winter had temporarily taken the profit out of beekeeping and driven the price to a dollar or a little better a hive, or stand as beekeepers say. Mr. Garner bought two thousand stands which he turned over to "Chunky" Woods, a good man with bees. Chunky nursed along the bees and the price rose to four dollars. When pecans were low Mr. Garner bought and stored them, often sending wagons into Mexico. Mohair, which comes from goats, dropped to seventeen cents a pound and Garner bought fifty thousand pounds which he sold at forty-one cents. He backed a young relative in the wholesale grocery business. He built a motion picture theatre. But the supreme test of John's genius for turning a dollar came when Clark, Fuller & Garner had a country newspaper dumped in their lap. If anything at that time had a poor record for money-making it was country newspapers taken as a class; and the Uvalde *Leader* was no exception.

Garner tackled the job as if born with printer's ink in his veins. A successful newspaper must first of all attract readers. John wrote conversation-stimulating editorials on subjects that touched the everyday lives of the residents of Uvalde County. His staff consisted of a printer and a youthful printer's apprentice. The printer was a bright fellow, as printers usually are. Garner got him to scour the town for news and get names in the paper—a hundred local names every week; what people were doing and saying. Then he spread canvassers over the county to show samples of the rejuvenated *Leader* and take subscriptions, paying them half of what they collected. Circulation went from four hundred to nine hundred and merchants found it paid to advertise in the lively medium. With the paper in the black Garner sold at a profit.

Mr. Garner's first investments were in mortgages. Then he acquired control of an abstract company and began a study of land titles along the Rio Grande. Some of the early grants ran into astronomical figures. In the early days English capitalists had invested heavily and then apparently written off their investments. Garner found some of those titles good. He would locate the English heirs and offer one or two dollars an acre for their holdings—which was just so much velvet for the English heirs and just so much velvet for John Garner who would sell the land for twice what he paid for it.

Garner always had cash at hand and had it where he could get it whether banks were open or not. During the 1907 panic when Texas banks were running on scrip John's real currency commanded fancy figures. His profit during that short crisis was between sixteen thousand dollars and seventeen thousand dollars.

Early in his career Mr. Garner began buying stock in local banks. When the Zavalla County Bank at Crystal City was in a bad way he bought a controlling interest at fifty-five cents on the dollar and made it worth three times par. In 1921 Mr. Garner owned also the First State Bank of Uvalde and had stock in twenty-six other Texas banks. During the money squeeze of that year several of these banks folded. Garner advertised that he would personally guarantee deposits of the two banks he controlled. Had either failed it would have taken his entire fortune, but his guarantee bred confidence and there was a run on neither. His liabilities as a stockholder in banks that were liquidated cost him in the neighborhood of seventy-five thousand dollars, which was the biggest loss Mr. Garner ever sustained.

With the exception already mentioned, Mr. Garner has never been in court on a private money matter. Considering that his fortune has been made by no major lucky or masterful stroke but bit by bit in ten thousand small everyday transactions, and considering the human weakness for misunderstandings where property is involved, this is an unusual fact.

In the summer of 1938 Acree B. Carlisle, a carpenter, was putting a fence around Mr. Garner's barbecue grounds. He got to talking about a house in Uvalde which he had built for a man with money loaned by the Federal Housing Administration. The Vice-President inspected the house and asked what it cost. Carlisle said three thousand two hundred and fifty dollars.

"Hell's bells," said John, "I could build it for less than that."

Luther L. ("Looseleaf") Davis, railway express agent and city councilman, asked Mr. Garner to build him a house to live in. Mr. Garner said he owned six houses in Uvalde and that Mrs. Garner, who had to look after them, didn't want any more. Looseleaf Davis kept after the VP who finally said to draw up plans, give them to Carlisle and tell him to keep the costs down because Garner was going to fix the annual rent at fifteen percent of the cost. The house cost one thousand seven hundred dollars and seventy-one cents.

Others came to Mr. Garner for houses. Carlisle and his building partner, Chester Blevins, talked Mr. Garner into an agreement to erect seven or eight houses. Josh Ashby, junior, president of Garner's First State Bank of Uvalde, was instructed to pay the bills. The houses cost from one thousand dollars to twenty-two hundred dollars, the twenty-two hundred dollar one being for the town dancing teacher, Mrs. Vondy, and included a studio for her classes. Mr. Garner says the reason for the difference in the costs of his houses and the FHA loan houses is careful buying. FHA people say the reason is because their houses are better. It is hard to believe that they are nearly twice as good.

Mr. Garner would rather discuss the financial problems of a young couple starting out than talk politics. His formula for financial independence boils down to a few maxims which he says anyone can follow: spend less than you make, whatever it is; never go in debt; learn to make investments or find someone who can make them for you. He keeps track of the financial progress of young friends; knows when they have their first hundred dollars put away and working for them, their first thousand dollars, and so on. He takes as much delight in watching their nest eggs grow as if the money were his own—and that is pretty close to rapture. Get enough young people, says Mr. Garner, to plan their lives in this way and there is nothing to fear about the country's going insolvent economically or haywire politically.

VI

LEADER OF THE OPPOSITION

VI

Leader of the Opposition

*W*HEN the casualties of
the 1920 cyclone were accounted for the Democrats found themselves with only one member
on the Ways and Means Committee ahead of
John N. Garner—former chairman Claude
Kitchen of North Carolina. Mr. Kitchen's death
in 1923 made Garner the ranking minority
member.

99

The long, uphill climb seemed over. Under the organization devised by Champ Clark the senior Democratic member of the Ways and Means Committee was the party's leader on the floor. But in this instance Finis J. Garrett of Tennessee claimed the honor by right of his standing on the Rules Committee which was senior to Garner's rank on Ways and Means. Though disappointed, Garner refused to enter an open contest against his Tennessee colleague. Garner's behavior won over Garrett's friends, making the Texan stronger in the party councils than he would have been had he won the leadership by a divided vote. Actually he was leader without title, but so tactfully did he exercise his influence that Garrett took not the least offense. In 1928 when Mr. Garrett left the House to make an unsuccessful race for the Senate John Garner was formally declared the head of his party in the House of Representatives.

The job of a congressional opposition is to harry the party in power—to obtain compromises representing the minority point of view and thus meet the ends of a democratic government. Sel-

100

Photograph by T. W. Spofford's Studio, Uvalde, Texas

THE GARNER FAMILY AT UVALDE, LISTENING TO THE ELECTION RETURNS IN 1932.
Left to right: Tully Garner, Mrs. Tully Garner, their daughter Genevieve,
Mrs. John N. Garner, Mr. Garner.

dom is the minority able to upset the majority, substituting its program for the majority program. This is the way things should be, for the majority party in Congress nearly always represents the views of a majority of our citizens. Yet Garner was able to substitute his program for the majority program in his first battle as general-in-charge of the minority forces in the House. He did it by rousing the country to the realization that, on the income-tax issue, the House minority represented the wishes of a majority of the people of the United States.

In 1923 the prestige of the late Andrew W. Mellon, Secretary of the Treasury, was perhaps higher than that of any other member of the Cabinet. He had handled his own wealth so advantageously that the impression was that the public's finances were safe in his hands; as indeed they were. Mr. Mellon was an enormously able financier in the Hamiltonian tradition, the basis of which is that when the rich prosper the poor prosper in their proper proportion—"their proper proportion" being rather small, to be sure. The Jeffersonian view is that the wealth of the country should be more evenly laid out—less for those already rich and more for those who are poor. A more perfect example of these opposed systems could hardly be found than in Garner's fight to reform the Revenue Bill of 1924.

The War over, under Mr. Mellon's administration taxes had been reduced in 1921, and in 1923 he announced the cheering news of further reductions. Tentative schedules were published, showing how much less the smaller earners, with incomes under ten thousand dollars a year, would have to pay. By these means a great public sentiment was marshalled behind Mr. Mellon's proposals. In December, 1923, the Treasury program was placed before the Ways and Means Committee in a bill drafted entirely by the Republicans. There seemed to be enough steam behind the bill to push it through in a hurry and get those reductions on the statute books.

Mr. Mellon's bill covered one hundred and eighty-six pages. Congress, and particularly the Democratic members, were being deluged with letters and telegrams to pass it. Under these circumstances Mr. Garner sat down to study the voluminous bill. Reductions for smaller earners were there—in the amount of twenty-five per-cent. The tax of a man earning between ten thou-sand dollars and twenty thousand dollars was to be reduced thirty percent. On earnings between twenty thousand dollars and eighty thousand dol-lars the reduction dropped to about twenty-five percent. Then it increased up to thirty-nine per-cent in the case of earnings of two hundred thou-sand dollars a year and above. Generally speaking the smaller savings would go to the smaller earners and the larger savings to the larger earners.

Garner opposed this. He contended that the greater reductions should go to the taxpayers with the smaller means, the smaller reductions to those with the larger means. This squared with his pioneering theories of the income tax.

"But," he told his Democratic colleagues, "you can't stop something with nothing. The Republi-cans have something. They promise considerable reductions. It's our job to show that, attractive as they are, they are unfair to the small man. We must show the country that sufficient revenue can be obtained by keeping the heavier burdens on those most able to bear them."

The Treasury Department's publicity had been clever and effective. The first announcement had contained detailed reductions on incomes up to ten thousand dollars only, the second announcement on incomes up to twenty-five thousand dollars. Until the bill was presented, with a strong popular demand for its speedy passage, nothing specific had been given out as to the reductions for the very wealthy taxpayers.

Working day and night Mr. Garner and the Democratic experts prepared a schedule of reductions, which differed from those in the Mellon bill as follows:

Taxable income	Garner reduction	Mellon reduction
Under $ 10,000	60 percent	25 percent
$ 10,000	53	30
$ 20,000	39	26
$ 30,000	30	24
$ 60,000	22	24
$ 70,000	18	26
$ 80,000	15	29
$100,000	12	33
$200,000	11	39

Mr. Garner pointed out that the Democratic rates offered greater advantages than the Mellon rates to 6,641,262 taxpayers while the Mellon rates were more beneficial than the Democratic rates to only 9,433 taxpayers in the very high income brackets. Garner insisted that his party's rates would bring in the required revenue, taking the bulk of it from those who were most able to pay.

The Treasury disputed this warmly. The Garner plan would disorder the national finances, it said. Mr. Garner's scheme was called socialistic. It would result in an enormous national deficit. In reply Mr. Garner pointed out that the year before, in his argument against the soldiers' bonus bill, Mr. Mellon had predicted a deficit of three hundred million dollars. Instead there had been a surplus of six hundred million dollars.

"Uncle Andy may not be the greatest Secretary of the Treasury since Alexander Hamilton," the Texan observed, "but he is the only one to miss his guess by nine hundred million dollars."

The Democratic leader insisted that Mr. Mellon's estimate of the "ruin" of national finances under the Democratic tax plan would be no more accurate.

When the Ways and Means Committee took up the Mellon bill a fortunate circumstance favored Garner. The Treasury rates were more than four liberal Republicans on the committee could swallow whole. They more or less sympathized with the Democratic view and in the end declined to subscribe, or subscribed with reservations, to the Republican majority report, drafted by the late Ogden Mills of New York, which sent the bill to the floor.

The bill was presented by the Republican chairman, the late William R. Green of Iowa, who announced as he arose that he would not permit interruptions from the floor. Garner followed. He began by saying he would pause to answer questions at any time. He was on his feet two hours, the longest appearance he ever made before the House. He was very considerate of Chairman Green, whom he knew did not personally approve of many of the features of the bill he was defending. Speaking without notes Garner showed a thorough knowledge of the encyclopedic bill under consideration—as well as of every other revenue act the Congress had passed since 1913. He answered intricate questions from memory, in the whole course of his remarks glancing at the bill before him only two or three times for exact figures. Garner's performance thrilled the Democrats and made a handsome impression on a growing group of liberal Republicans.

The debate lasted two weeks. Garner was on his feet day after day. Section after section was taken up, amendment after amendment introduced. A number of votes were taken on amendments, the most important being the vote to substitute the Garner tax schedule for that of Mr. Mellon. Mr. Garner won by 221 to 196. Later the Republican leaders maneuvered a reconsideration of the question and this time Garner crushed them by a vote of 258 to 153. The Texan was leading a larger group of progressive Republicans all the time. The final vote on the bill, which embodied most of what Garner had fought for, was 408 to 8.

As the years went on Mr. Garner continued a thorn in the side of the Treasury Department.

His fight against the enormous income-tax re-
funds the department made to wealthy indi-
viduals and to corporations created national
attention. Leaders of Mr. Coolidge's administration and leaders in Wall Street denounced him as
an amateur at finance, a demagogue striving to
undermine the foundations of our "New Era of
permanent prosperity." Efforts to retire Mr.
Garner from Congress increased, and in 1928 the
Insull utility interests of Chicago sent money into
his district to beat him. In the election that followed Mr. Hoover carried Texas for the Republican national ticket but Garner was re-elected to
serve his fourteenth term.

Notwithstanding his effectiveness as an adversary and much which on the surface might pass
for bitterness, an important thing about John N.
Garner has always been his ability to get along
with the opposition. The characteristic first came
to notice in his pinfeather days when, practicing
law on the West Texas frontier, he would sit
down with counsel for the opposite side and nego-
tiate an agreement, saving a court trial. Garner's
appearance at Uncle Joe Cannon's poker game
and his friendship with young Nicholas Long-

THE PRESIDENT AND THE VICE-PRESIDENT AT THE JACKSON DAY DINNER,
WASHINGTON, JANUARY 8, 1939.

worth marked the beginning of this kind of thing in Washington. As Garner matured in experience more and more young congressmen applied to him for advice on the problems which afflict a junior statesman. They found nothing pontifical or highfalutin in the way the veteran dispensed his wisdom.

"Young man," he would say, "I want to stay in Congress every damn' bit as bad as you do."

One could at least credit the sincerity of a man who talked like that.

Republicans as well as Democrats came to him, and today the walls of Mr. Garner's office in Washington and of his library in Uvalde are studded with the mementoes of appreciative Republicans. There are autographed photographs of Cannon, Longworth, Fiorello LaGuardia and others, one of which bears this inscription:

"To John Garner. With good wishes in every possible direction except politics. HERBERT HOOVER."

The friendship between Garner and Longworth became a celebrated affair in the capital about which has collected a library of typical Washington "inside" stories. Once when Garner appeared on the floor of the House after a serious illness Longworth, then Speaker, called for three cheers. Another time, in a convivial speech before the Alfalfa Club, Garner nominated Nick for president—on the Republican ticket.

Without sacrificing party advantage or prerogative on either side of the House their cooperation speeded routine legislation. The membership of the House is four hundred and thirty-five, but under adroit leadership twenty men can put through an essential bill and, in general, control the program of the House. As the group must be bi-partisan its activity works to the public advantage by eliminating useless delays and pointless oratory. Keeping its plans secret an unofficial bi-partisan steering committee can circumvent the pressure groups which otherwise would flood Congress with letters and telegrams giving a false appearance to popular sentiment and, as frequently has happened, inducing weak-kneed congressmen to vote against their convictions.

LEADER OF THE OPPOSITION

When Longworth was Speaker and Garner minority leader this situation led to the establishment of what was colloquially known as the Board of Education. The quarters of the Board were in an obscure room reached by a tunnel-like passage branching off the stately corridor which forms the thoroughfare between the House and Senate wings of the Capitol. That corridor is lined with statues and the "tunnel" comes in just at the left of the statue of Stephen F. Austin. Nick equipped the room with an icebox for cooling fizz-water. For this Garner had no use, preferring to thin down his rye with "branch water," or the nearest thing to it in the Capitol, which is water from the tap.

After a day's session Longworth and Garner would pass the word to a few of their respective lieutenants such as Bert Snell of New York, John Tilson of Connecticut, Sam Rayburn of Texas and John McDuffie of Alabama. Neither Mr. Longworth nor Mr. Garner being preaching or practicing prohibitionists, the company would enjoy a few minutes' relaxation from the day's grind by "striking a blow for liberty." Then the legislative program for the following day would be taken up. If trouble was feared from a member of either side he would be sent for and the little caucus would begin its active function as a Board of Education.

This co-operation with a Republican Speaker to put through without fuss or delay the routine legislation which keeps the wheels of government turning brought no favors to John Garner from the Republican national organization. There was probably no other Democrat in the House that the Republican national committee would have rather seen beaten. Garner was one of the few congressmen of either party who had to meet opposition from outside his district at election time.

On the way home from a Board meeting Nick would drop John off at his hotel. They rode in the Speaker's official automobile which Garner always referred to as "our" car, admonishing Longworth to take good care of it as he, Garner, would be using it pretty soon. Next morning some matter of party principle, or advantage, might inject itself into the proceedings on the floor of the

House. Garner would be on his feet in two seconds, and the fight between the two friends and their followers would be no pillow fight. The Board of Education operated only in support of a theory which Mr. Garner long has enunciated, namely that eighty percent of our national legislation should be approached in a non-partisan spirit.

When the election returns of 1930, so disastrous to the Republicans, were coming in, Mr. Garner received the following telegram from Cincinnati:

> WHOSE CAR IS IT
> N L

He responded:

> THINK IT MINE WILL BE PLEASURE TO
> LET YOU RIDE

At the moment, Mr. Garner was mistaken about the car. Longworth retained possession of it by virtue of a very slender majority for his party in the House. Before the new Congress

113

was organized, however, there were several deaths, including that of Longworth himself. In the special elections to fill the vacancies the Democratic swing continued. In December, 1931, when the Seventy-second Congress was organized the composition of the House stood:

Democrats	218
Republicans	214
Farmer-Laborite	1
Vacancies	2

John N. Garner of Texas was elected Speaker. The New Era of permanent prosperity was over; the depression was in its third winter; the bread lines were lengthening. The instruments of democratic government were confronted by a serious test. Mr. Garner was to preside over our most representative and volatile body, one-third of whose membership had been freshly elected by a confused and sometimes bitter people. A good many of the Democratic newcomers owed their seats to the espousal of the fantastic remedies of relief which spring from the minds of a depressed and desperate electorate. They came to Washington with a dozen inflationary and printing-press money schemes. This was the body Garner was to lead, the only body in the government controlled by his party. The Senate remained Republican and Mr. Hoover was President. Garner would have to lead the House with a plurality of only four and a majority of three. A misstep would set the stage for legislative chaos.

VII

SPEAKER OF THE HOUSE

VII

Speaker of the House

ON MONDAY, October 6, 1931, Mr. Garner was taking his ease at his home in Uvalde, on the shady back porch which overlooks the barbecue pit and a pecan grove, when Birdie May, the colored cook, placed a telegram in his hands:

I AM ASKING LEADERS IN CERTAIN COMMITTEES WHO MAY BE IN REACH TO MEET WITH ME AT THE

MR. GARNER OF TEXAS

WHITE HOUSE AT 9 OCLOCK TUESDAY EVENING
NEXT UPON AN URGENT NATIONAL MATTER   I AM
ANXIOUS THAT YOU SHOULD COME   IN ORDER TO
AVOID HARMFUL SPECULATION I SHOULD DEEPLY
APPRECIATE IT IF NO INFORMATION OF THIS CALL
SHOULD BE GIVEN OUT   I WILL BE GLAD TO PLACE
A PLANE AT YOUR DISPOSAL IF YOU DESIRE
                                     HERBERT HOOVER

Uvalde is two thousand miles from the capital. An Army plane flew down from San Antonio. Mr. Garner got in and fourteen hours later he touched the ground again at Bolling Field, Washington. It was his first ride in an airship, and he has never taken another.

Mr. Hoover had prepared the ground for his meeting by a series of secret conferences with financiers and economists inside and out the government, among them Bernard M. Baruch. The White House meeting, which began at nine in the evening, lasted until midnight. Present were thirty-two senators and representatives, Andrew W. Mellon, Ogden L. Mills and Eugene Meyer. Mr. Meyer was chairman of the Federal Reserve Bank board, Mr. Mills, Undersecretary of the Treasury and the real power in that department. The President was looking for a post into which to retire Mr. Mellon gracefully and soon was to find one in the ambassadorship to the Court of St. James's.

The President asked for a united, non-partisan attack on the crisis. He outlined a program, the main object of which was to thaw frozen assets, expand credit and start money circulating. He proposed:

1. Organization of a private five hundred million dollar revolving fund by banks to loan to lesser banks outside the Federal Reserve system to loosen credit. In this he had already received promises of co-operation from the heads of great banks in New York and other large cities.

2. Governors of Federal Reserve banks to make advances on the tied-up securities of closed banks in their districts so that dividends might be paid depositors at once to help them over a hard winter.

In addition Mr. Hoover proposed three measures which would require legislation:

121

1. Broadening the provisions of the Federal Reserve acts to enable Federal Reserve banks to rediscount paper not at that time eligible for rediscount.

2. Increasing the capital of the Federal Land banks to provide more money to loan to farmers.

3. Creation of "a Finance Corporation similar to the War Finance Corporation" to make loans to private industry.

The Democrats present promised to support legislation making possible these measures.

"Politics," said Mr. Garner, "will be a secondary consideration. Country should always come ahead of party and now the country should be the sole thought of everyone."

When Congress convened on December 7 the crisis had tightened. A "hunger march" on Washington of unemployed men was in full swing. Amid these scenes Mr. Garner was elected Speaker. Responding to a complimentary address by Bertrand H. Snell, the defeated Republican nominee, he said in conclusion:

122

"I made no promises to secure this preferment and I have none to make now."

This plain talk was addressed to the Speaker's Democratic colleagues. Mr. Garner had, however, made a promise to the country to support the White House conference legislation. He kept it— in face of the fact that on the day he took the oath as Speaker five thousand other bills were introduced, all worthy in motive, perhaps, but some of them embodying about every crackpot scheme of miraculous government finance under the sun. Garner swept them deftly aside. He reconstituted the Board of Education, kept his slim Democratic majority in hand and in the course of a few weeks the bills creating the Reconstruction Finance Corporation, increasing the capitalization of the Federal Land Banks and liberalizing the rediscount authority of the Federal Reserve were passed.

Garner's work as an adversary of Andrew Mellon's theories of taxation had given him a certain country-wide prominence, lifting him out of the category of influential congressmen who are unknown to the country. His work for the emergency program placed him on the plane of contemporary national figures. Mr. Hoover consulted Garner almost as often as he did his own party leaders. On Washington's Birthday, 1932, House Republicans joined the Democrats in a rousing demonstration for the Speaker. Tourist guides in Washington began to receive requests to be shown through the offices of John N. Garner. It being a presidential year the Texan was paid the customary compliment of mention as a possibility for the party nomination.

So far so good. Then came the Revenue Bill, which to balance the budget had to yield $1,246,-000,000. A measure was reported by the Committee on Ways and Means, raising old taxes and instituting new ones. The bill represented a compromise between the Democratic and Republican leaderships. It ignored the multiplicity of fancy schemes whereby prosperity should be restored, with plenty for all, at practically no cost to anyone. This was more than the coiners of such schemes could stand. With a tremendous uproar they bolted the committee bill, breaking

Garner's grip on the Democrats and Snell's grip on the Republicans. Irregulars on both sides of the chamber began to tear the bill to pieces. Taxes estimated to raise half a billion dollars were sliced away.

For ten days the House was a sight to behold. There was no organization worthy of the name. Wall Street stock and bond prices dipped still lower. Government securities began to slip. The Democrats being the majority party, Garner was on the spot. His newly-won prestige began to fade. He was told he had to save the Tax Bill, or some tax bill raising the required revenue.

On March 29 Garner surrendered his gavel and descended into the well of the House. As usual he spoke without notes. There is nothing of the conventional orator in Mr. Garner. But this time there was a deadly earnestness in his voice that compelled attention at the outset.

"I think more of my country than I do of any theory of taxation that I may have, and the country is in a condition where the worst taxes you could possibly levy would be better than no taxes at all.

125

"You have expressed yourselves. You have arrived at a conclusion that you will not have a sales tax. I have no quarrel with you because of it. I appeal to you not only in the name of my party but my country that in view of the fact that there has been stricken from this bill more than five hundred million dollars of taxation, it is your duty, your paramount duty, to restore some taxes to this bill in order that the country's financial integrity may be maintained. . . .

"I believe that if this Congress today should decline to levy a tax bill there would not be a bank in the United States in existence in sixty days that could meet its depositors. . . ."

The old country banker paused to let that sink in. Then he did something reminiscent of the religious camp meetings he had attended as a boy on Blossom Prairie.

"I want every man and every woman in this House who . . . is willing to try to balance the budget to rise in their seats."

The applause did not come for several seconds. It started small and grew in volume as all but a few members stood on their feet.

126

"Now," said Mr. Garner, "if they do not mind, those who do not want to balance the budget can rise in their seats."

No one rose.

Bert Snell took the floor to ask, very solemnly, that Republicans carry out their pledges "to our very distinguished Speaker."

Before the day was over the House had adopted taxes totalling one hundred seventy million dollars or about a third of what was needed.

Arthur Krock, political expert of the New York *Times,* wrote of the day's performance:

"Rarely in the annals of parliaments has the intervention of one member in a crisis disspelled it so promptly and so effectively as did Speaker John N. Garner's address to the House." Summarizing the results—the House on record for a balanced budget; the authority of leadership restored; the insurgents "shamed"—Mr. Krock concluded: "For one speech these are enormous achievements."

In a few days the remainder of the deficit was made up and the bill passed.

The Hoover relief program—Mr. Garner never

liked to hear it called that, though the initiative was the President's—the Hoover relief program was on the books. It was a start but only a start, as experience has shown. At the time there were clamors for more immediate measures to diminish the army of thirteen million unemployed. In the House thought was definitely developing in favor of a huge public works program, easier government credit to business, particularly small business, and an attack on the agricultural surpluses.

In May Mr. Garner introduced a bill calling for an outlay of two billion three hundred and nine million dollars:

1. One billion two hundred and nine million for a federal public works program to be expended on public buildings, mostly post offices, and highways, waterways and flood control projects.

2. A billion dollar increase in the capitalization of the Reconstruction Finance Corporation for loans to private corporations and to states, cities and towns for public works; and for loans to finance the export of farm surpluses.

Photograph by Dr. Erich Salomon

The Vice-President and His Wife

3. One hundred million dollars to be expended at the discretion of the President.

Mr. Garner would levy a gasoline tax of a third of a cent a gallon to pay for this.

The bill created an explosion which, as far as the White House was concerned, ended the party truce which had held since December. Mr. Hoover denounced the Garner proposal as the greatest pork-barrel scheme conceivable. He said its enactment would destroy the credit of the government. Ogden Mills and others chimed in. Mr. Garner called this a poor return for the Democratic support of the White House conference program. In reality he was not greatly disturbed because a national campaign was at the country's doorstep and the truce could not have lasted much longer anyway. Besides, the shrewd old Texan knew he had a lot of Republican support in Congress for his plan.

The Garner bill quickly passed the House and the Senate. President Hoover vetoed it, and this seemed a political act. Promptly Congress adopted a substitute measure embodying much of

129

what Garner had asked for. This became a law.

Meantime Mr. Garner had received his reward in the form of the vice-presidential nomination. During the campaign he delivered one speech only, despite all the pressure that could be brought to bear. To one importuner he told the story of the Texas ranger and the riot.

It seems that when only one ranger showed up at the seat of disturbance someone frantically inquired:

"What, just one ranger responded to our call?"

"Just one riot ain't there," observed the ranger.

Privately Mr. Garner assured Franklin D. Roosevelt:

"Hoover is making speeches, and that's enough for us."

VIII

THE VICE-PRESIDENT AND HIS WIFE

VIII

The Vice-President and His Wife

ANY sketch of John N. Garner requires some space devoted to his wife. Etty Garner has had an important share in her husband's success, and she is one of his mainstays now. During his thirty years in the House she continued as his secretary. When elected Vice-President a time-tried friend advised him to release Mrs. Garner from official duties that she

might give her time to the social obligations de-
volving upon the Second Lady. The dignity of
their new position, the friend said, demanded it.

Mr. Garner has never been much on the brand
of dignity that has to display a silk hat to be
identified as dignity. Yet he appreciated the sincerity of his friend's counsel. Tears stood in his
eyes when he said:

"I want to do what is right in this new job. But
people will have to take me as I am; and that
means taking Etty, too. We've been partners
too long. I couldn't do without her."

The last wish of Mrs. Garner would be to relin-
quish her work as her husband's almost invisible
alter ego and give over her life to the incessant
round that is official Washington society. Thirty-
six years ago she came to the capital, a young wife
who liked pretty clothes and a good time. She
had seen a good deal more of polite society than
her husband who had never been in a city larger
than San Antonio. She bought John his first dress
suit, accepted all the social invitations that came
their way and thoroughly enjoyed herself.

In those early days Mr. Garner's official duties

were slight and his correspondence small. Mrs.
Garner says that her work as her husband's secretary was no more than any woman needs to do to
keep out of mischief. This did not last. Garner
began to rise in the party counsels and with the
coming of the Democrats to power under Wilson
in 1913 he had real work to do. Mrs. Garner, in
complete charge of the internal administration of
the office, was equal to the occasion.

Without a good secretary a congressman's mail
can wear him out. Unless that mail, most of which
does not amount to a hill of beans, is carefully
answered people back home feel hurt and pretty
soon there will be a hole in the political fences
that an aspiring rival can drive a heap of voters
through. John Garner had more than a good secretary; he had one of the best. Nine-tenths of the
letters that came to his desk he never saw. And
in larger matters of politics Mrs. Garner became
her husband's most trusted counsellor.

As the work increased Mrs. Garner had to de-
cide whether to give up her secretarial job or to
curtail her social program. She decided to curtail
the social program and, although she says she did

not appreciate it at the time, this was the wisest and most far-reaching decision of her life, next to her marriage. Had the decision been otherwise Mrs. Garner might have become one of Washington's important hostesses, for she has the qualifications. Instead she has become one of Washington's important persons.

Mariette Garner is a grandmother—an easy-to-know, very sensible and very pleasant woman. She is one of the best-informed and certainly she is the least-publicized of women in Federal government circles. She is also one of the most envied. Washington wives whose names are household words have laid their heads in Etty Garner's lap and sobbed hysterically over the emptiness of their lives.

Shortly after the 1932 election a woman said to Mrs. Garner:

"I suppose you'll give up your office work now."

"And do what?" rejoined the Second Lady-elect. "When I give up office work I'm going back to Uvalde and stay there."

Leaving Mrs. List's boarding house in 1906

the Garners took two rooms in the Burlington Hotel, near Thomas Circle. As Tully grew up, these quarters expanded to eight rooms; they wanted a place where their son could bring his school friends. When Tully married the Garners scaled down their living quarters in the capital. Now they have three rooms in the Washington Hotel and usually eat breakfast and dinner in the coffee shop. Mrs. Garner often prepares lunch for the staff and herself on an electric stove in the Vice-President's office. She says she cannot bear to give up housekeeping altogether.

The Garners have reversed the precedent which made the vice-presidential couple Washington's most persistent diners out. They are the capital's rarest diners out. The only official function on the regular calendar the Garners attend is the President's dinner to the Cabinet. The only one they give is the Vice-President's dinner to the President. Mrs. Garner entertains the Senate ladies at a luncheon each year. One or two party affairs like the Jackson Day dinner and one or two Washington fixtures like the Gridiron Club dinner complete the Vice-President's schedule.

MR. GARNER OF TEXAS

Five nights a week the Garners are in bed by ten, usually after playing a few hands of rummy. At five-thirty they are up and at seven-thirty in the office. Secretaries and clerks appear at eight and by eight-thirty callers begin. The morning mail brings about a hundred letters. By nine Mrs. Garner has them read and sorted and has begun to dictate the answers. In the evenings the Garners used to like to take in an early movie, but since the 1940 talk started the Vice-President has not been able to appear anywhere without a crowd gathering. Consequently he spends most of his evenings in his apartment, reading or talking to friends who leave at nine-thirty. If they do not the Vice-President says, "The place is yours," and prepares to turn in. The Vice-President's favorite reading is American, modern European and Roman history. Of late, however, Mrs. Garner has been buying her husband western and historical romances of the Zane Grey brand for relaxation. In Uvalde they go to the Strand Theatre three times a week which is as often as the program is changed. In Washington, as in Uvalde, Mr. Garner takes a siesta after lunch—or dinner as he is apt to call the midday meal.

Back of the Garner home in Texas, a low-lying, two-story, oak-shaded brick house showing the Spanish influence, is the four-room frame cottage in which Mr. and Mrs. Garner started housekeeping. Two rooms are filled with cases containing Mr. Garner's correspondence and other official papers for the period of his forty-odd years in public life. Another is the bedroom of Uncle Augie (August) Rheiner, Mrs. Garner's bachelor half-brother. The other is John's private office. But most of Mr. Garner's business in Texas, political and private, is transacted on the back porch of the main house or on a bench by the barbecue pit.

His outdoor pastimes are the same as they have been for fifty years—hunting and fishing. A public man cannot always choose his company, even for hunting or fishing. When important strangers to the Rio Grande country show up to fish with the Vice-President they go out in dude style. A hunting picture of Mr. Garner has been published showing him dressed like a Metro-

139

Goldwyn-Mayer version of a Maine guide on Sunday. But when Mr. Garner goes fishing to enjoy himself with Ross Brumfield or some of the other Uvalde boys, any member of the party could pass for a desert rat.

Ross Brumfield is an automobile mechanic who has prospered sufficiently to own a garage and a repair shop. He knocked down an old Ford for Mr. Garner and built a trailer. This Garner likes to hitch to a pre-depression Chevrolet, re-upholstered with a deer hide, and light out for the Rio Frio to be gone a week. Unless it rains, which is seldom in West Texas, the Vice-President sleeps on the ground. The trailer is fixed up like a cow-outfit chuck wagon and Mr. Garner can throw together a mess of biscuits which those who have eaten them say melt in your mouth.

When Mr. Garner became Vice-President he told the newspapermen he was through talking for print.

"I'm a member of a firm—the junior member. Go to headquarters for the news."

Off the record he added:

140

THE VICE-PRESIDENT AND HIS WIFE

"I'm not going to turn out like Charley Curtis if I can help it."

Charley Curtis was Mr. Garner's predecessor in office and his friend. There was no more genial soul on Capitol Hill than Charley Curtis until he left the floor of the Senate to preside over that body. Then he got pompous all over and began to think his views important. The views of Mr. Curtis had not been very important as a senator; as Vice-President they were something less than that.

Mr. Roosevelt's first six months in office witnessed the launching and the establishment of the New Deal. In the opinion of this writer no peacetime president since Jackson has inaugurated a program destined to have so lasting and so profound an effect on the future of this country; and I say peacetime president merely to avoid a comparison with Lincoln, which would lead us rather astray. If the history of sociological progress teaches us anything, a generation hence this country will be following paths blazed by Franklin D. Roosevelt in a dire hour in our national life.

The Speaker of the House of Representatives

141

handles a gavel of mallet-like proportions. The Vice-President manages his nominal duties as moderator of the Senate with a little cylinder of wood about the size of a kitchen salt-shaker. The office of Speaker holds potentialities of great power and strong men have made much of this. Though his speakership was short and the times unusual John Garner proved himself a strong man in that office. The vice-presidency is the most curious post in our governmental structure. It was not designed for power, and able men, like Calhoun, have tried to be powerful in it to their sad embarrassment. A score of lesser men have gone the way of likeable Charley Curtis.

John Garner is one of the few who have grown in stature in the office. Mr. Harding introduced the custom of having the Vice-President sit with the Cabinet and offer his views. Mr. Harding's Vice-President was Calvin Coolidge. The practice was followed through succeeding administrations and we had General Dawes and Mr. Curtis at the Cabinet table. Mr. Roosevelt continued the custom and John Garner has sat with the Cabinet since 1933. Perhaps he has said less at those meetings than any of his predecessors, excepting Mr. Coolidge, but what he has said has counted for something—in and out of government circles.

In the early days of Mr. Roosevelt's administration Garner re-constituted the old Board of Education, using a room on the second floor of the Senate Office Building. There he summoned senators and representatives who were slow to perceive the excellence of the President's program. Much early opposition to the New Deal was melted away in that informal atmosphere. The late Senator Nate Bachman of Tennessee called the room the Dog House and when a legislator was "in the Dog House" his colleagues were pretty sure that he would stay on the New Deal reservation.

The Dog House fell into disuse after 1936 when Mr. Garner began to doubt the wisdom of the President's continued spending policies. I have heard congressional leaders say that the President's real difficulties with Congress began when John Garner discontinued his "educational" work. The President's Supreme Court reorganization bill, in early 1937, and the sit-down strikes provided further points of disagreement between the Vice-President and his chief. Though Mr. Garner held to his policy of reticence the fact of these differences became well known, for Mr. Garner understands the uses of silence as well as the uses of publicity. The strike and the court issues have settled themselves. On the policy of spending Mr. Garner and the President still differ. The Vice-President's differences on this head with some of the President's latter-day advisers have been described as violent. Nevertheless Mr. Garner continues to attend Cabinet meetings and on other matters his advice at times is sought by the White House and cordially given.

Not since Jefferson held the office has a Vice-President been so influential as Mr. Garner. The fact seems to have changed him little. His office— the actual rooms—are a sort of corner-store forum and John Garner is as approachable, as salty of tongue and as short on formality as ever. To Washington in general he is "Jack" Garner— about the only exceptions to this rule being the

CAMPING ON THE RIO FRIO

© *Harris and Ewing*

Mr. Garner's favorite recreation. The Vice-President is usually the camp cook. His companions are Hub Oeff and Ross Brumfield, the proprietor of a garage in Uvalde.

people who have known him longest and best. To them he is John or Mr. Garner. "Cactus Jack" and "Texas Jack" are newspaper inventions entirely—however useful at campaign time they may prove to be. Around Uvalde the Vice-President is simply John. Down there John means John Garner. Other Johns are John Smith, John Martinez and so on. This quiet mark of respect is the more noteworthy when one considers the shirt-sleeves manner of the man to whom it applies.

Mr. Garner's elevation of a traditionally dead-end office to one of the strongest in the land has given rise to the Garner Legend. The approach of an election year is always a good time for legends, especially in the case of a man who is running for president. So we have the Garner Legend.

"Yes," say the skeptics, "and we had the Coolidge Legend, too."

True; but with this difference. A review of the record would seem to suggest that the Coolidge Legend was mostly legend and the Garner Legend is mostly Garner.

INDEX

INDEX

149

INDEX

INDEX

153

INDEX

155

INDEX

Rivers and Harbors Bill, the, 40-41

Roosevelt, Franklin D., 130, 141, 143

Roosevelt, Theodore, 46, 58

Rutherford County, Tenn., 13

St. Louis, Mo., 64

San Antonio, Texas, 29, 30, 31, 120

Senate
  Democrats won, 65
  Garner bill passed, 129

Seventy-second Congress, the, 114

Sherman, James S., 49

Sims, Capt., M. L., 17

Snell Bertrand H., 111, 122, 125, 127

South, the, 14, 83

Starr County, Texas, 39

Statuary Hall, 50

Sugar Trust investigating committee, 63

Supreme Court, the, 67, 68

Taft, William Howard, 41, 61

Texas, 90
  anecdote of, 11, 12
  boundary of, 15

Texas—*cont.*
  machinery of government in, 25
  people knew of Garner's work, 43
  saying about, 32

Texas Legislature, the, 31, 32, 44

Tilson, John, 111

Treasury Department, the, 104-105, 107

Treasury program, 102-103

Tremont House, 39

Tumulty, Joseph P., 72

Underwood, Oscar, 67, 68

Underwood Tariff Bill, 67

United States, the, 46
  census figures for 1900, 34
  financial collapse of 1837, 12

United States Court of Claims, 47

Uvalde, Texas, 18, 19, 23, 28, 37, 58, 89, 91, 109, 119, 120, 138

Uvalde *Leader*, the, 91, 92

Valls, Judge John, 39

Vanderbilt University, 17

Victory loan, 70

157